SERPENT LOVE

A MOTHER-DAUGHTER EPIC

by

Penelope Scambly Schott

with a response by Rebecca Kramer

For my daughter

perhaps I have loved you too hard

Scientists now inform us that post-childbirth some
of the child's cells remain forever inside
the body of the mother

A cow gave birth to fire. She wanted to lick it but it burnt her tongue. She wanted to leave it, but she could not because it was her own child.

– Ethiopian proverb

CONTENTS

Poems by the Mother

Striped Cowl

The woman spent years knitting her daughter a cowl.
Now she is knitting a pair of mittens to match one row
of the multi-colored striped cowl. Knit purl knit purl.

If the new mittens match the brightest stripe, her hands
will rise like fireflies, but if they match a darker stripe
her hands will swim invisible as fishes in a clouded lake.

So, what color is the yarn? A color no one can name
because she knits these mittens inside a magic bag
from the cobwebbed attic of fear. If you call this *failure*,

you have misread her future.

Attachment

I want to take you to that narrow place in my life
where I almost didn't make it through,

to the front hall, the heavy door, the pillared porch,
to how there was or wasn't a moon that night,

to how the physical beating heart
can feel injured unto breaking,

and I want to leave you there
to remember your own doorways

where someone you loved beyond reason
decides he no longer loves you,

and now my daughter is in that narrow space
where a tall, blond man has closed the door,

and I don't feel her pain in my heart
but below my heart where the slick

and twisted umbilical once attached
to my unforeseeing womb.

My Married Daughter Phones at 2 a.m.

Suddenly I am her mother again.
I knew
she couldn't stay with him,
and I also knew
she didn't know how to leave.

I turn back into my younger self
back when I wished
my lover still loved me,
when I desperately wished
I didn't still love him so desperately.

For the woman I was then,
I will rescue her.
For the broken woman I was back then,
I will say, *Do this, then do that.*
I will give birth to her and all her boxes.

I will do this because I believe in miracles.
I believe the great etched slug
with its quivering eye stalks
will spy the far side of the street
and I believe the slug will arrive there

glistening.
Oh, my sad daughter,
let me be the mother I wanted to have.

The Mother Drives All the Way Out to Gresham

She has driven for miles past adult-only shops and
check-cashing services

to collect the settee her divorcing daughter
picked out on craigslist.

Now she chomps her whole Gala apple, core in-
cluded, and tosses

the stem down onto the floor mat with every other
unswallowable thing

from her ordinary and complicated life.
The directions stink.

Forty-seven circling miles later, the mother gives
up, drives home without

the fancy carved Victorian settee.
Back in California,

in her soon-to-be ex's home, the daughter is cradling
two small dogs,

the Pomeranian she will bring to Portland
and the old, blind Maltese

she may never see again. The daughter is the baby
with whom this mother

had the easy labor.

4

The Reverse Side of the Tapestry

I was glad she was coming here.
I hunted up a cute condo by a park.

It was a city park where couples hung out.
She cried over her angry ex-husband.

The park had a dog park.
The dogs were too big for her Pomeranian.

She didn't like the ritzy neighborhood.
I wanted her to be safe.

She didn't like my self-satisfied city.
She didn't like her life.

I wanted her to be happy.
I wanted her to be happy.

No, I wanted *me* to be safe.
No, I wanted to be done mothering.

Failed Rescue

For eighteen months she stayed in our city.
For eighteen months she lived in the condo.
For eighteen months she dated local dudes.

For eighteen months I ran errands with her.
For eighteen months her stepfather took her out to dinner
and tried to help her unpack boxes.

The angry ex- kept mailing her more boxes
while the little dog peed on the floor, Oh.

On the Day After She Moves Back to California

I scrape the condo floor: bits of pastry,
used Kleenex, q-tips, smashed kibble.

Next I hire a disaster-cleanup company.
The boss sniffs and then asks, *Ferrets?*

No, I say, *un-housebroken dog.*
His guys use shovels and a plastic barrel

until nothing remains but soap and a rag—
one frayed square from some childhood towel.

I am wiping away her miserable months.
I dip and squeeze the thin rag. I wipe filth

and tears from my face. In scalding water,
I rinse that red rag clean.

Anger Party

Ah, Anger, I should throw you
a party. There will be a bouncer,
with a buzz cut and lightning tattoos.

The guest list will be highly restricted.
Understanding and Forgiveness
will be turned away at the door.

Dear Anger, I've spent my whole life
preparing for this party. All those years
I kept mistaking you for grief—

the way you hid in my bed
or behind the eyes of my daughter.
Well, Anger, it's time to step out in public

and enjoy your goddam bad-ass party.
Shoot up the place. Scratch up your face.
Nice job, Anger. How good did *that* feel?

So, Didja Know

that an ant can lift 50 times its own weight
that a jack rabbit can travel more than 12 feet in one hop
that a bee has 5 eyes
a slug has 4 noses
a whale has 2 penises

that a snake really does have hip bones

and that for every human mother in this world
there are approximately 2 chickens?
So, hey there, buddy,
ya wanna take 1 of my chicks?
Cheap? Cheep.

Curriculum Vitae

At the local high school, she didn't do her homework. At boarding school she got suspended two weeks before graduation. I made her ride five states home on the grey dog. Along the way she stopped to visit her father. He died a month later. When she had told him she wanted to be an actress, he said, *Well, you won't make it on your looks.* Back then, she was so beautiful it hurt.

She landed the female lead in one movie made for British television. She kept attending auditions. She extra'd. She tried out for voice-overs. She moved to California. She quit. She did manage to get one of her dogs featured on local t.v.

She dropped out of four different colleges, the last one a community college in Santa Monica. She knows a lot. I don't know how much it annoys her that her brother is a tenured college professor.

She collected serial boyfriends and at last married one of them. I made finger sandwiches. Her two little dogs were flower girl and ring bearer. I felt such relief knowing that she was married.

He started drinking and threw her out. I bought her a condo in my city and paid for the move. She hated my city. Everything wrong with my city was my fault. She moved back to her city.

Now she writes underpaid articles and quizzes for an internet site. One quiz went viral. I sent her $500 at Christmas. She waited two weeks to open the envelope.

10

She dates gorgeous young men while shopping for someone her own age with a good vocabulary. But the older guys still think they want to start a family.

She is brilliant and funny, she is tiny and cute and loving, she is almost fifty.

Notice how these paragraphs get shorter.

Dream of Abdication

A lion cub crouched in each corner
while a wolf whimpered at the window

My dead parents insisted on watching
through invisible walls

My middle-aged daughter lay in her bed
under the sweet white headboard

Her world was bewailings and yes-buts
My world was made of trying

My clawed hands lunged for her neck
The room smelled meaty and foul

My mouth tasted like rubber and iron
behind my bitten lip

I opened my eyes to a blood red sky—
tail lights burning in midnight mist

My husband snored and the dog snored
while I tallied up my sins

I swallowed both halves of a sleeping pill
without disturbing husband or dog

I awoke the next morning centuries older
and no longer her mother

My Claws

For many centuries
the Sphinx's great paws

were buried in sand drifts.
Her claws are still invisible.

Like mine. I've been agreeable
for seventy years.

When you visit my house,
I offer tea in floral cups.

My Victorian Nana
taught me to fold napkins

into linen fans,
but nobody taught me

to swipe
with my blunt fingernails.

Any day now
I'll turn into an old she-wolf

whose teeth and claws
can rip through hide.

I will scratch out the eyes
that saw or didn't see me.

(continued)

You might need to know this:
the practical claws of a wolf

can never retract. Nothing
can be unsaid.

The birds of sorrow

stand too long in tall grass,
and they will build their nests
in your uncombed hair.
With small twigs,

they will pick, pick at your scalp until
they unweave your cap of misgivings,
and give you up to pure despair.
A thousand sorrows

swoop and hover over bent grass.
For every clump of grass,
there are many sorrows
and each sorrow

is named *sorrow* or *bunch-grass*
or *flyaway-grass* or *broken thing*.
Winds rise until your eyes burn.
Each sorrowing bird

is your fragile daughter flying
beyond your brooding. Your eyes
shut and open, open and shut.
You see too much.

Around you in frozen grasses
fall all the feathers unpreened.
You say *Dear bird, I am tired—*
come peck my eyes blind.

**How sharper than a serpent's tooth it is
to have a thankless child**

What makes me teary
are the charming moments

like after supper in the red kitchen
of early childhood

when her big brother could read
but she knew more words,

and he looked up from his book
to ask, *What's a serpent?*

That's easy, she told him,
tilting her head in her sunbonnet.

*A serpent is someone
who works for somebody else.*

I have been her serpent
for almost fifty years

or she has been mine.
Our blood hisses together.

16

August Night

The woman among pear trees
listened for silence.

The small bones of her ears
felt the pears growing.

She lay in cool grass
between orchard rows

where stars lowered
their small strings.

From time to time,
she plucked those strings.

One pear dropped.
She heard it thump and roll.

The wind stopped.
Crickets paused.

What if her world is an orchard
bearing unspeakable things?

Or was her name *Mother*
before she had words?

Story of the Beautiful Daughter Ralinavut

A woman had a beautiful daughter.

Our daughters are always beautiful.

A wolf pack came to their village.

When the daughters are old enough,
the wolves show up.

The daughter left with the wolves.

This is not unusual.

The mother mourned.

What else would a mother do?
Wouldn't you mourn too?

After three years, the mother went looking.

Took her time, didn't she?

*She ran like a wolf to the far North
and found her daughter living with wolves.*

Here comes the part I don't understand:

The daughter Ralinavut ran home with her.

*They arrived as wolves and scared the villagers
before they turned human and walked in snow.*

Nothing in the story about Ralinavut
after she was no longer so beautiful.
Nothing about the wolves she left.

And nothing at all about my daughter
who lives so far off to the South.

Short Course in Self-Improvement

Stand up and throw your burdened shoulders back.
It might save your spine from getting bent out of shape.

And isn't it time to clean out the inner junk drawer?
You'll never find the mate to that old black glove of rage

or if do you, it will be full of dried-up mouse shit.
But most important, stop apologizing.

You are a mother so everything *is* your fault
which is why you must meditate daily upon armadillos

who have managed to stay soft under their hard shells.
You could do worse than an armadillo.

Now let your daughter pat the brown spots on the backs
of your hands. They are forming new constellations.

Lesson

I went to the petrified forest
and was disappointed:

beautiful mineralized trees
but none of them standing erect.

The stone forest I had imagined
raised jeweled trunks to the sky.

Now I am learning to remember
every magnificent scene

I ever invented: cool shade
of those tall stone trees

where I sit with my daughter
warming our two stone hearts.

Because my first kid was a boy

I was surprised and thrilled
to give birth to a daughter

I fell in love with her fingernails
and her dark curls

We picnicked by the millrace,
boy, girl, and mommy

I sliced a fat red apple
into six sections

while my girl hopped rock to rock
beside the river bank

announcing, *My whole real name
is Apple-jumpy-climber*

If I could travel to that afternoon,
maybe I wouldn't

Dahlia

Sometimes I like to say *dahlia dahlia dahlia* even though
it isn't my favorite flower but I love how it lies on the
      tongue
like *darling darling* like my daughter who used to be tiny
and hopeful and now heartbroken at forty-seven she still

calls me *Mommy* as if it were my permanent job to mend
her life even though I've been loving her so damn hard
for almost half a century and that's why I want to reread
Joseph Conrad and ask him—beg him—plead with him—

to tell me: *Is it important to be heroic?* because as long as
I keep on being *Mommy* I am also the Captain going down
with the ship and I think how instead I should be rescuing
the *deserving* poor—as if anyone ever *deserved* anything—

and then I give up and simply pronounce *dahlia dahlia*
and my dog looks up at me as if I have told her something
important and I wonder is it too late to rename my
      daughter
because if I called her *Dahlia* maybe we could start again.

Why I Like Snakes

They are clothed in jewels
They are muscular
They shed the past

From the used skin of a snake
a dreamer can invent
translucent wings

The woman who meant well toward the world

She asked permission before embracing
the thundercloud plum tree. The tree, birdless,
said *yes*.

Striations in the bark reminded her
of her own familiar flesh, how skin loosened
and blew into ridges.

The woman worried about using up the world.
What if she ate all the persimmons or wore out
the verbs? *caress, adore, wink*.

In the wink of her eye, all the years disappeared
or reappeared with the childhood Irish setter
or box elder beetles climbing a sunny wall.

This was her question: Was it too late,
had it maybe always been too late,
to donate her amazements to her grown children?

And then she saw it—
how this world she cherishes is one of many,
and only this one hers:

the sofa cushions,
the charred scum of the coffee pot,
this April sky so busy with ducks.

Portrait of the Mother as a Late Learner

When she had nowhere to go, I invited her
to move here. I told myself a pretty story:

It will be white and lacy.
She will invite me over for tea.
I will show her off to my friends.

A year and a half, she never unpacked.
I paid for her move back to Los Angeles.

Now she has unpacked, fixed up her room
by the freeway. Feeds me delicate goat cheese.

Joy, joy to my daughter in her new home.

Every Woman's Mother

Every woman's mother is a witch
Every woman's daughter is a warrior

Every girl's mother has learned to slither
like a boa constrictor among men

Each mother picks a smocked snake skin
her daughter is eager to shed

Snake mother with her pointed fangs
then poisons the daughter

always hoping

the daughter will circle back in the dark
to play her unwrinkled fingers

through her human mother's white hair

Rapunzel's Mother
A Response by Rebecca Kramer

I want to be named Dahlia and start again. I didn't keep going to auditions like my mother wrote. I only got two after making the movie. I got a callback for one and a job from the other one. I didn't have the right connections or looks to get auditions. Maybe Dahlia did.

In California I appeared repeatedly on reality TV; apparently I had the right looks to be me. I did it because I could bring my little dog with me. I wanted the footage of him I didn't have of my father who died when I was 17. I've always envied movie stars' children their footage of them.

My ex, like my mother's ex, was tall and blond, but not beautiful anymore. He drank or embittered that away. And he wasn't my mother's ex; he broke my heart in his own right. But he was a good dog parent. When I moved to Portland I took Isabel, my girl dog, with me and left Spike, my little boy dog, with him. Just like my mother took me and initially left Daniel, my brother, with my father when he left her. Then later, like my mother, I took him back.

I'd left Spike with the man once my husband, because Spike, though a little fluffy dog, was a man's man. The one kind thing my ex did for me after we separated was maintain a twitter feed for Spike, so I could see pictures and hear what furniture Spike had marked that day. When I got Spike I did the same thing for him. "Tell your mother, blah, blah, blah." "Tell your father, blah, blah, blah."

As Spike got older and sicker he needed a mother more than a father so I came and took him to Portland. My ex told me I didn't love Spike, but he must have known I did or he wouldn't have let me take him. Does that mean he didn't mean the other harsh things he said to me either?

When Spike joined me and Isabel, my Pomeranian, in Portland we trashed my mother's apartment, Rapunzel's mother's tower, together. Just we three. Sometimes it was tidy, but never when my mother, the witch, stopped by without notice. And my belongings, gifts from my husband when he loved me, filled the tower from the turret to the dungeon, the little basement under the foundation.

I tried to love that home my mother provided but I couldn't. It remained a bad hotel or Sartre's *No Exit.* When I separated from my husband I told her I wanted a home and she magically produced one. But what I didn't understand was that the home I wanted was the one I'd had in LA with him.

And while I was in Rapunzel's tower my hair grew white, not long, so there was no escape. Except very briefly, when I was rushed to the hospital with kidney failure. I had told my mother's expensive doctor I was sick, but he'd believed the tests, not me. The emergency room believed me and the new tests were in my favor. I slept in the hospital for three days, healed through the arm by antibiotics. It was the only time spent in Portland that I ever felt safe. While I was there my mother slept for three nights in the pretty tower bed she'd bought me, with my two little dogs to make them feel safe. I cherish my mother and my dogs for the time they slept together.

When I was released from the hospital, my mother confronted me about the state of the tower I'd left suddenly. I was still sick for the next couple weeks and hallucinated her swinging towards me as I slept, poised to attack. I'm too rational to hallucinate fully awake. I only do it on the fringes of sleep. I tried to sleep less even though for months it was dark, and I only knew it was morning from the clock.

I had dinner with my stepfather on weekends. I love him and enjoy his company, but I had dinner with him because I understood that my Portland rent was babysitting my stepfather while my mother was away at her writing house. She loved that second house and hated me for not visiting it, but I'd hoped to make peace with the house she put me in first. I didn't. It wasn't the beautiful tiny apartment I'd shared with my husband.

I didn't blame my mother for her city. I blamed her for not knowing it. She invited me there to open a doll hospital. I fix antique dolls. I can make new limbs from clay. My father lost his limbs before he died, so shaping new ones is very satisfying. There wasn't a need for this skill in Portland. The only old doll I ever saw there for sale was just a doll head and it had a plant growing out of it.

I took my dog children to the dog park she found across the street twice a day. It kept me from going more insane, but I feared for my little dogs' safety among the giant hiking companions that roamed like Titanosaurs in mud. I wondered if I was doing the right thing for my children or putting them in danger for my sake. I go to dog parks like other people go to bars to pick up a conversation. The grass around the mud was dead, because Portlanders are too politically correct to water and I missed the wasteful green of the parks in drought-ridden LA.

I needed to find someone else to love, but the men in Portland wore beards more often than jobs and invited me to endless pubs but never paid for my diet Coke. And the man who had a job, a white collar one, paid for two Kahlua and Crèmes, then raped me when I fell asleep. I woke up part way. In the morning he asked me to marry him. My mother didn't want to hear it or see the pleading letter of apology he wrote. She told me to instead tell a friend.

When my little boy dog got still sicker, the vet in that ritzy neighborhood wouldn't see him. She was too busy so she referred us to an emergency vet and was angered when I pointed out the thousand dollar difference. I nursed Spikey on my own, with the expensive air filter my mother bought so my and my puppy's allergies to the pervasive mold and wet plants wouldn't be so bad. When I started to breathe audibly I went to a doctor with my soon to be ex-husband's insurance, but he had stopped paying it so my mother had to. The doctor told me I would always have allergies in Portland and the only way to fix it was move. I couldn't yet.

Age and coughing caught up with Spike. My mother and stepfather ordered the finest doctor in the land and she gently put him in to sleep in my mother's little tower. He died cradled in my stepfather's arms because he was happy with him and so I could look at him one last time. He liked men, which is why I initially left him with his father, but my stepfather surrogated. The vet offered us a towel so Spike wouldn't soil laps when he died, but his loving mother had walked him first, so he didn't have to.

32

My little dog smiled, kissed my stepfather, kissed me when I leaned in, then drifted off to sleep. Spike died more gracefully than any Victorian child, and I scattered his ashes in the dog park in the Northwest, talking to him as I did it, letting him know he would always be loved.

When Spike's ashes were scattered, because I didn't want to bring him back to LA as dust, I took Isabel, my girl dog child, in my arms and we escaped with pieces of the jewels and computer hardware my ex-husband had given me. We left everything else and my mother's tower in shambles, bolted the door and didn't look back. There wasn't time to fix it, I had to get out.

I moved back to LA, to the tiniest legal apartment imaginable, but an apartment not a room. My landlady and building manager check in on me and my little girl dog to make sure we're safe living up against the freeway. They had a birthday party for Isabel in the building office.

I have the apartment thanks to the blood alimony that gave my ex-husband his excuse to hate me and my mother who nursed me from her wallet of adulthood till the alimony came. I'm paid on the high end of the scale for writing Internet articles and quizzes but it isn't enough, even to get by poorly on.

I go out with smart, beautiful young men and look for an old man for whom I'm not too old. It will work; I still look sort of like a little girl. It's either God's mercy or his sense of humor. What I'm looking for is my next husband/parent because my mother shouldn't have to take care of me and even as a child I knew I'd be bad at taking care of myself.

And in the meantime I mother the homeless old lady down the street. I research social services for her, I pack her little packs of goldfish crackers and I wash her dog. I wake her in the morning like somebody's mother so she gets to her social service appointments. I believe we will all eventually be someone's mother, because it's easier than taking care of ourselves.

Nostradamus, a postlude

Even in the chapel
I knew I shouldn't be marrying him

but I wanted babies
and he had almost finished his degree.

All these years later my kids understand
that they really shouldn't exist,

but over the phone last midnight
my uncannily psychic daughter

announced with complete conviction,
I still would have known you.

Even if you hadn't married him,
you would have been my mother.

Thanks to the following journals for publishing some of these poems:

Natural Bridge, "The Woman who Meant Well toward
    the World"
Naugatuck Review, "Curriculum Vitae"
The Passaic Review, "Dahlia"
Rhino, "Story of the Beautiful Daughter Ralinavut"
The Sourland Review, "My Married Daughter Phones at
    2 a.m."
Watershed Review, "Anger Party"

And especially thanks to my daughter Rebecca Kramer for reading and responding to these poems. Sometimes writing can re-connect people.

Penelope Scambly Schott is a past recipient of an Oregon Book Award for her verse biography of Puritan rebel Anne Hutchinson, *A Is for Anne: Mistress Hutchinson Disturbs the Commonwealth.* She has published three other verse narratives about women in history. Among her many other books, the collection *Crow Mercies* received the Sarah Lantz Memorial Award from *Calyx.* Her newest is *How I Became an Historian* and forthcoming is *Bailing the River.* Her chapbook *Lovesong for Dufur* honors the small central Oregon town where she now spends part of every week and where she teaches an annual poetry workshop. In the past Penelope has worked as a cosmetics salesgirl at Macy's in Herald Square, a donut maker for Scrumpy's cider mill in New Jersey, an artist's model for art groups and classes, a home health aide for the elderly, and mostly as a college teacher. A mother and grandmother, she lives with her husband and the white dog who owns them – the same dog who helps to host the White Dog Poetry Salon, an ongoing series of readings by invitation in their Portland home.

Contact www.penelopescamblyschott.com.